Denver and Rio Grande Railroad Company

Valleys of the Great Salt Lake

Describing the Garden of Utah and the two great Cities of Salt Lake and

Ogden

Denver and Rio Grande Railroad Company

Valleys of the Great Salt Lake
Describing the Garden of Utah and the two great Cities of Salt Lake and Ogden

ISBN/EAN: 9783337073053

Printed in Europe, USA, Canada, Australia, Japan

Cover: Foto ©ninafisch / pixelio.de

More available books at **www.hansebooks.com**

VALLEYS

OF THE

GREAT SALT LAKE

DESCRIBING THE GARDEN OF UTAH

AND

THE TWO GREAT CITIES

OF

SALT LAKE AND OGDEN

ISSUED UNDER THE AUSPICES OF THE PASSENGER DEPARTMENT OF THE
DENVER & RIO GRANDE
AND
RIO GRANDE WESTERN RAILROADS

CHICAGO
R. R. DONNELLEY & SONS COMPANY
1890

Full information how to reach Utah, with rates of fare, etc. will be cheerfully furnished upon application to

F. A WADLEIGH, Ass't Gen'l Pass. Agent, D. & R. G. R. R.

DENVER, COL.

W. B. COBB, Gen'l Eastern Agent, D. & R. G. R. R.

317 Broadway, NEW YORK.

J. W. SLOSSON, Act. Gen'l Agent, D. & R. G. R. R.

236 Clark Street, CHICAGO, ILL.

L. B. EVELAND, Trav. Pass. Agent, D. & R. G. R. R.

105 Ninth Street, KANSAS CITY, MO.

W. F. TIBBITTS, Trav. Pass. Agent, D. & R. G. R. R.

DENVER, COL.

A. N. OLIVER, City Pass. Agent, D.& R. G. R. R.

DENVER, COL.

W. H SNEDAKER, Gen'l Agent Pass. Dept. R. G. W. Ry.

No 14 Montgomery Street, SAN FRANCISCO, CAL.

PREFACE.

THE one fact that everybody knows about Utah is that it is the seat of the Mormon Church, beyond this the majority of people have never sought to investigate. The vast improvements wrought by the industrious and frugal pioneers of Utah, the great natural resources of the territory, the balm of its health giving and invigorating climate, the wonders of its majestic mountains, the sylvan beauties of its unrivalled valleys, the new relations of amity and progress that have sprung into life between all the religious sects of the territory, and especially in Salt Lake City, the enterprise of energetic railroads, the building of great irrigating canals, the establishment of manufactories, the growth of mining, in short, all those great strides towards absolute pre-eminence, which Utah has made, have been to a great extent ignored in the past. It is to correct this mistaken judgment, or rather to give facts upon which a correct judgment may be formed, that this little book has been written.

There is no line of argument so convincing as a calm and judicious presentation of facts and figures. Eloquent phrases may please the fancy, fervent rhetoric may touch the heart, but dispassionate and truthful words alone can convince the judgment. It is to the judgment of the reader that the present work is addressed and therefore fact has been given the precedence of fancy, and no statement has been ventured that can not be fully sustained by mathematical demonstration. This being the case further comment is unnecessary, and this little book is submitted as a frank statement of fact for judicial consideration.

SALT LAKE CITY.

CHAPTER I.

GROWTH OF UTAH TERRITORY.

WHEN in 1847 the leaders of the Mormon People settled in the Great Salt Lake Valley and began the up-building of this valley and its great central city, they little dreamed of the future possibilities of their new home. It was not long, however, before they began to realize that the resources and possibilities of this wonderful country far exceeded their most sanguine expectations and accordingly, under the leadership of Brigham Young, (who was an organizer and an executive officer with abilities of a degree which merit the admiration of all persons,) was laid the foundation for a city, upon a scale which is to-day the admiration of all who visit it. They laid out that city in blocks, 660 feet square, with streets 132 feet wide. Along either side of these streets were planted shade trees, which now make Salt Lake a lovely city in the summer season, with the streams of water running down either side of these broad avenues and a splendid system of water works, fed by pure fresh mountain creeks. Beautiful drives in the spacious Parks excite the admiration of all. The whole city, with its rich lawns, fragrant flowers, gardens and stately shade, is one veritable bower, nestled at the foot of a range of mountains whose picturesque grandeur enhances the beauty of the scene.

But Salt Lake City will be fully described in succeeding chapters, and it is concerning the Territory of Utah that we wish to speak now. During the first quarter of a century after the arrival of Brigham Young and his followers, they were substantially the sole occupants of the Territory. They knew there were minerals in the hills, but preferred to devote themselves solely to agricultural, horticultural and manufacturing pursuits. The knowledge got abroad, early in the seventies, however, and resulted in the influx of a host of miners and prospectors who meantime have become a part of the permanent population. Under the supervision which Congress exercises over a Territory, causes of alienation and strife between the Mormon and Gentile have to some extent been outgrown, removed or placed in process of removal and extinction. The relations of the two classes have softened, and with the passing years are growing fraternal instead of antagonistic.

Within the last two years the desirableness of Utah, considered as a place of residence, has apparently for the first time dawned upon the people. The subject has become the favorite theme. Schemes for the improvement of so fair a heritage and for making known its advantages abroad, involving the co-operation of all classes, have come in vogue, and associations of business men have been formed in the principal towns to give direction and support to local ambition and effort in the direction of both moral and material advancement. To the visitor, to all who are seeking new homes, these associations present Utah as in many respects the most inviting field left open for occupation to-day.

The population of Utah is estimated at 215,000, of which nearly if not quite one-third are non-Mormon. The assessed valuation for 1888 was $46,379,969, about 40 per cent of the real value, namely, $115,949,920. Add to this 20 per cent for mines, which are not taxed, and it appears that property worth $139,139,984 has been created in Utah in forty-one years. The products of the Territory for 1888 are fairly estimated as follows (first two items not estimated):

Gold, silver, lead, copper, Salt Lake prices	$ 7 557,241
Coal, 253,000 tons, $2.10 at the mines	531,300
Agricultural and horticultural, about	8,000,000
Dairy, eggs, poultry, etc., about	1,000,000
Increase of live stock at 30 per cent	5,000,000
Wool, 9,000,000 lbs. at 12c per lb	1,080,000
Lumber, hides, and pelts, salt, brick	1,000,000
Other manufactured articles, about	5,000,000
Total	$29,168,541

BEE HIVE HOUSE.

The total land area is 52,501,600 acres; water area, 1,779,-
200 acres. The Uintas, the Wasatch, and the High Plateaus,
constitute a considerable part of the total area. The Territory
is exceedingly interesting, geologically, and has been very
thoroughly examined, mapped and described, by the Powell
Survey. In 1877 officers connected with the Survey measured
the streams and the lands they can be brought upon, and cal-
culating the irrigating duty at 100 acres per cubic foot per
second, limited the irrigable-arable lands to 2,262 square miles.
Later estimates place the area at 3,000 square miles. A certain
40 square miles in Valencia, Spain, under the canals of the
Turia, sustain 70,960 souls. At one-fourth of this density of
population, our 3,000 square miles would sustain 1,323,000 souls.

Major Powell estimates the timber region at 18,500 square
miles; standing timber at 10,000; milling timber at 2,500 square
miles. The timber is sufficient, he says, for the industrial wants
of the country, if it can be protected from the fires started by
the Indians to drive the game. Since Major Powell wrote, this
has been practically accomplished by the removal of the Indians
to reservations.

The grazing lands lie between the high timber lands and the
low farming lands. The grass is scanty but nutritious. The
minimum area of a pasturage farm in the best pasturage lands
Major Powell places at 4 square miles. Wherever grass grows,
he says, water may be found or saved from the rains in sufficient quantity for all the herds that can live on the pasturage.

About 13,000,000 acres have been surveyed to date. Per-
haps one-fifth of this area, inclusive of 15,000 acres of coal and
1,500 silver mines, has been disposed of under the various land
laws. About 500,000 acres are cultivated.

Although crops are grown in favorable localities without irrigation, yet irrigation is indispensable to the Utah farmer.
With the acequias made, watering costs at the outside $3.50 an
acre. At the same time it enriches the land and assures a full
crop. Civilization is indigenous only in rainless countries where
man controls seed time and harvest. Any farmer in the world
might well choose to do his own watering (if he could) rather
than be subjected to the capricious skies which bend above the
" humid " region.

In no part of the Union are all sorts of minerals found in
greater variety and abundance than in Utah. Coal is mined on
both fronts of the Wasatch and of the High Plateaus from the
Uintas to the Colorado River. The yearly output exceeds 250,-
000 tons and might as well be ten times that. The coal beds
are sufficient to supply Utah and all the region west to the
Pacific for generations.

Remarkable bodies of iron ores occur in Iron County, and

MORMON TEMPLE, TABERNACLE AND ASSEMBLY HALL.

ordinary deposits in sundry localities, some of them, as analyses indicate, Bessemer ores.

There are practically illimitable fields of brimstone, ledges of rock salt, antimony and cinnabar mines, and in Great Salt Lake an inexhaustible storehouse of salts and chemicals There are indications of oil and gas in Green River Valley, reefs of sandstone saturated with asphalt, veins of black pitch (gilsonite), stringers and bunches of natural paraffine (ozokerite), mineral resin, and other rare and curious hydro-carbons.

The yearly output of the Utah lead-silver mines is about 165,000 tons of ore, four-fifths of which is reduced in Utah mills and furnaces; the product worth, at seaboard prices, about $10,000,000. All over the Territory are found the best of structural and fertilizing materials. Nothing but capital is needed to double the mineral output both in value and variety.

It will be seen that Utah has been bountifully endowed by nature, and that man has made very good use of his opportunities. The people as a rule own their little properties. These are not heavily mortgaged as in the " humid " region. There is no respect in which the condition of the dwellers in the mining part of the " arid belt " is not superior to that of the people occupying the purely agricultural States. Diversity of pursuits is the occasion of this superiority. On no account would the men of the " desert" exchange places with the men of the prairie, but they are willing the latter should come out and share their advantages. The " frontier " was jumped as it were from the Hundredth Meridian to the Pacific; it is now returning upon its course, this time on the ground instead of in the air. The ever advancing tide from the East is now met by a reflex tide from the West, and the meeting place is in the longitude of Salt Lake Valley.

CHAPTER II.

SALT LAKE CITY.

SALT LAKE CITY is one of the most beautifully located cities on this continent. It possesses elements of beauty in such variety and of such superior character as are not to found in any other one city in America. To the tourist, the pleasure seeker, health seeker, or to the man of means who is looking for a new location or for a place in which to make an investment, Salt Lake City presents greater attractions than are to-day presented by any other growing city of the United States. There clusters about Salt Lake City matters of historic interest, which are peculiar to herself, and will always be a source of interest to all classes of people.

When the emissaries sent out by the Mormon Church, after their removal from Illinois to Missouri, returned to their people and reported that in the discharge of their work they had selected as their future home the wonderful Valley of the Great Salt Lake, they rendered a service of inestimable value, for which they should ever be rewarded with the grateful remembrances of their own people, and also of the Gentiles, who have since learned to appreciate the wisdom these emissaries displayed in making the selection which they did. Without doubt there is no place where there can be found such an harmonious intermingling and blending of the elements which constitute a foundation for the up building of a prosperous country with a great central Metropolitan City as is exhibited in this great Inter Mountain Country, consisting of Utah, Western Colorado, Northern Arizona, Nevada, Idaho, Eastern Oregon and Wyoming, with Salt Lake City as the natural, the established and the assured Railway, Commercial, Financial, Manufacturing, Educational and Social Center. That Salt Lake is without a doubt (and without a rival) the

TRAMWAY IN LITTLE COTTONWOOD CANON.

Metropolis of this vast and productive section of country, which is yet in its infancy, is a truth which is self evident.

To the seeker for health, pleasure or profit there is no more attractive point than Salt Lake City. From out of the foot of the Wasatch Mountains, which form the background of the picture just presented, flow numerous thermal and mineral springs, whose medicinal and curative qualities have long been, and are constantly being, practically tested by invalids from all parts of the United States. Hundreds of the present residents of Salt

Lake City, who came here in search of lost health, are to-day living, sound in body and in health, testifying to the wonderfully beneficial results of the springs, the baths and the climate of Salt Lake City, which latter for lung and bronchial troubles is pronounced by eminent authorities to be unexcelled, and by a gentleman who has made a close study of the subject and whose observations are based upon practical experience with cases in Salt Lake City, her climate is very highly recommended for people afflicted with heart disease or troubles of a nervous character. The bathing at the various warm and hot springs possesses wonderful curative properties.

Members of the leading religious societies or organizations can find here, in flourishing condition, the' representative churches, and strong congregations of their respective sects. The talent in the pulpits as well as the services and the music of our various churches, are up to the standard of eastern cities. A place of great interest to all people, whether of a religious turn of mind or not, is the great Tabernacle of the Church of Latter-day Saints of Jesus Christ, or, as it is ordinarily termed, the Mormon Church. Each Sunday afternoon at 2 o'clock this immense structure, which is one of the largest auditoriums in this country and possesses acoustic properties unequalled by any other structure in America, is crowded to its utmost capacity, which is 13,462. It is 250 feet long, 150 feet wide, 90 feet high, oval-shaped, with an arched roof unsupported by columns. This is the largest span of unsupported wooden roof in the world. The interior construction is so perfect that the dropping of a pin can be heard in any part of the immense auditorium. The grand organ in the Tabernacle, the second largest in America, has 3,000 pipes, and is used as an accompaniment for a well-trained choir of 200 voices. Large numbers of Gentiles attend these services. In the same square of ten acres, is the Temple, a beautiful structure of native gray granite. The corner stone of this building was laid April 6th, 1853. The structure is 200 feet

long, 99 feet wide, and has cost up to date three and one-half
million dollars, and will require a million more to finish it.
The Assembly Hall in the same block is also of white granite;
it is 120 by 68 feet, has a seating capacity of 2,500, cost $150,-
000 and has the most elaborately decorated interior of any
building in the West. The Endowment House, where the
marriage, baptism and endowment ceremonies were performed
previous to the completion of the Temples in the Territory, is
there in the same square. The Lion House, opposite the
Amelia Palace, was known as the residence of ten of Brigham
Young's wives. It is located in the same block with the Bee
Hive, which was Brigham Young's Executive Building of the
Church. Next to this is the President's office. The Tithing
House, where are collected the tithings, is in the same block
with the Bee Hive and the Lion House. Across the street in
front of the Bee Hive is the Amelia Palace, or the Gardo
House, which was built by Brigham Young as a residence for
his favorite wife, Amelia Folsom Young. The Eagle Gate is
an archway surmounted by a large eagle, and spans First East
street, or State Road as it is called. Fort Douglas is a Regi-
mental Post situated three miles east of the center of the city,
and is at an elevation of about 400 feet above the city proper.
The site is beautiful and affords a lovely view of the entire
valley, city and lake. The post and grounds are regularly
irrigated and accordingly kept in beautiful condition.

   The Warm and Hot Springs are located in the north part
of the city and are grealy prized for their wonderful curative
qualities. Water from these springs is piped to the city, where
splendid baths are provided in a large Natatorium, centrally
located.

   At the Chamber of Commerce, which has temporary rooms
while waiting for the completion of its new building, there is to
be seen a very fine collection of the mineral, agricultural, manufacturing and other resources of the Territory of Utah and the
City of Salt Lake. Any one desiring to procure a proper idea

ENTRANCE TO OGDEN CANON.

of the variety and extent of these resources and the future possibilities of Salt Lake City and Utah, or who may want any printed or illustrated matter concerning the City or Territory should not fail to visit the Chamber of Commerce at No. 71 West Second South street.

As was before stated Salt Lake City is one of the best amusement and theatrical cities of its size in the West, and supports two first-class theaters, the Grand Opera House and the Salt Lake Theater, which are occupied almost constantly by the very best organizations that cross the continent.

Other points of great interest are the Z. C. M. I. boot and shoe and other factories, institutions which have grown up and are highly creditable to the city. The magnitude of these institutions is ample evidence of the extent to which any and all lines of manufacturing may be developed here for supplying the vast territory tributary to Salt Lake City.

Salt Lake is noted for being one of the best hotel cities in the country, and in order to meet the rapidly growing demands of the traveling public there are now under construction two immense hotels of three hundred rooms each, which will cost half a million of dollars apiece.

There are in successful operation in this city manufacturing establishments of the following character: Boots and shoes, knitting and overall, silk, woolen and paper mills, tanneries, confectioneries, fence and mattress factories, cracker factories, show case makers, stone works, brick yards (with splendid quality of clay for building, for fire and paving brick, in inexhaustible quantities) aerated water works, roller grist mills, cigar factories, vinegar factories, soap factories, salt refining works, chemical works, glass works, wooden work establishments, printing, book-binding, lithographing, brewery, etc., etc. The statistics taken in 1887 show that over five thousand employes were engaged in these various industries. There are splendid fields here in all lines of manufacturing which have been found profitable at any of the manufacturing centers of the East.

The wholesale business of Salt Lake City was in round numbers last year six million dollars. This, like the manufacturing business, presents a splendid field for development in any department to be mentioned.

Outside wholesalers are just now beginning to appreciate the fact that Salt Lake City is destined to be the next great commercial center in the westward march of empire, and almost daily new mercantile enterprises are being established either on a retail or a wholesale scale, and numerous firms engaged in the retail business are branching out as wholesale establishments.

As to her public improvements Salt Lake City is far in advance of many other cities of her size in the East. Besides having an inexhaustible supply of pure and wholesome water, she has one of the most thorough systems of electric lighting, both arc and incandescent, to be seen in the United States, all of her streets being brilliantly lighted all night.

In addition to a very complete telephone system, consisting of over five hundred instruments, the city has an American District Telegraph messenger service.

Her gas plant supplies a good quality of gas at prices usually prevailing in cities of her size. In addition to the present company there is now applying for a franchise a company which proposes to furnish gas for light, fuel and power purposes at a very low degree, so low in fact that it will be cheaper for manufacturing and domestic purposes than soft coal, of which latter, by the way, there is an inexhaustible supply and of very superior quality to south and east of Salt Lake City. For smaller manufacturing institutions, such as do not care to invest in separate power plants, or for large ones who find it more profitable to utilize a cheap power furnished by electricity derived from the utilization of the immense water power found in the mountain streams emptying into the Valley of the Great

OGDEN RIVER.

Salt Lake, there is now being perfected a company which will
put in plants to develop many thousands of horse power for
distribution throughout the city

The street railway system in Salt Lake City is as thorough
and efficient as could be desired anywhere. The latest im-
proved electric lines are in successful operation on twenty-two
miles of track belonging to the Salt Lake Street Car Company,
which is soon to replace with electricity its eight miles of horse
car lines yet in use. With its extensions to be made in the
immediate future and the construction of the electric lines by
two other companies, Salt Lake City will have, by the end of
1890, no less than fifty miles of splendidly equipped electric
street railways.

There is now nearing completion a splendid system of sewer-
age, consisting of over eleven and a half miles of sewers.

Active operations for paving the principal business and residence streets of the city, have already begun, and the contracts
are now let for paving of the best character upon other streets,
which will mean the employment of a vast amount of labor and
the substantial development of the city.

For the residence portions of the city there is in contemplation a plan by which the centers and sides of Salt Lake's broad
avenues will be parked, seeded down to blue grass and set in
trees with paving on either side of the center strip of parking.
The electric light, telephone, railway wires are all strung on
poles placed in the middle of the broad streets, between the
double car tracks.

The city authorities have ordered and are now using a large
number of new sprinkling carts in the business and residence
portions of the city, making the streets most delightful for
driving.

Among other metropolitan features which Salt Lake City
possesses, her extensive fire alarm system and very efficient
steam fire department are not to be omitted, nor is her well
disciplined, finely uniformed and highly creditable police force,
which would soon amount to sixty men. Her health department is a very efficient one.

CHAPTER III.

SALT LAKE CITY AS A RAILROAD CENTER.

SALT LAKE is the best provided with railway connection of any city of this Inter Mountain country, as it has direct railway connection with all the railroad towns in the territory indicated; not only is this the case, but there are at present in an advanced stage of development, railroads from Salt Lake City to San Diego, California, to Los Angeles, California, and one direct to San Francisco, California, and another in contemplation, north along the west side of the Great Salt Lake into Idaho, which will give her competing lines into all portions of her tributary Inter Mountain country. All of the Inter Mountain lines of the Union Pacific railroad have been consolidated as the Oregon Short Line and Utah Northern, with general offices at Salt Lake City The general offices of the Rio Grande Western, which is now standard gauge its entire length, and forms a link in the Great Trans-continental Trunk line, have been removed to Salt Lake City, where are also located its extensive shops.

The Salt Lake and Fort Douglas, the Salt Lake and Eastern and the Utah Western are all narrow gauge roads which diverge from Salt Lake, distances are from twenty to fifty miles, with contemplated extensions much farther, now open for direct communication, Salt Lake City and numerous splendid mining localities tributary to her.

In the matter of development Salt Lake City is progressing at a rate and with a degree of solidity not to be witnessed in any other city of her size. On the 15th of April there were in actual construction (to say nothing of almost as many more decided upon or in contemplation) no less than twenty-seven business blocks and manufacturing establishments, whose total

IN SPANISH FORK CANON.

cost will be $2,625,000. In addition to this amount there is
now being expended no less than one million dollars for
private residences. Taking the business and public buildings
(excluding a new city hall and court house costing two hundred
thousand dollars) the manufacturing establishments, the
various public improvements, the street railway extensions, the
railway construction and other forms of improvements, there
will be expended in Salt Lake City during the present season
not less than six million dollars in the way of permanent
improvements.

There has already passed the U. S. Senate a bill appropriating five hundred thousand dollars for a federal building in this city, and the matter is now pending before the House.

With the successful efforts now being put forth by Salt Lake City's lively and energetic people, to secure manufacturing and other enterprises, which will materially develop and establish upon a firm and substantial basis, the metropolis of this Inter Mountain Country, there is now no better city in which to make either a location for residence, for health or for business, or where money can be invested with greater safety and more certainty of good returns than in Salt Lake City.

Contrary to the ideas which have apparently prevailed in certain sections of the country, the people of Salt Lake are of very sociable and very thrifty character and invite new acquisitions in business and other lines. In this work the Gentiles, who are now in the majority, are united with the Mormons.

For persons seeking investments in mining properties, in agricultural lands, in stock, or in the grazing business, the country immediately tributary to Salt Lake City cannot be equalled.

The mineral wealth of Utah and its adjacent states and territories is comparatively unknown and practically undeveloped. Almost daily for the past sixty days there have been filed with the Secretary of Utah, articles of incorporation for some new mining enterprise, which makes its headquarters in Salt Lake City.

As the wealthy mine owners, stock raisers, etc., of California have made their residences and spend their money at San Francisco, and the similar classes of Colorado do the same at Denver, just so do the mine owners, stock raisers, speculators and investors of this whole Inter Mountain country come to Salt Lake City to reside, to secure the best opportunities for educating their children and to enjoy life from the profits of their very lucrative properties.

OGDEN CANON NEAR POWDER DAM.

Salt Lake City is just now entering upon an era of substantial development in her business and permanent improvements and steady growth in her realty values, which promises to carry her forward without interruption, as less bountiful resources in a very short time developed and made Denver what she is and all she promises to be. Salt Lake's prospects are even brighter than were those of Denver, for the reason, that when Denver was Salt Lake's present size, the means and the methods for the rapid growth and development of cities were not so thorough nor so quick in their results and benefits as are those with which Salt Lake is now adequately provided. Her railway connections both east and west, north and south, far exceed those which Denver enjoyed at a corresponding

period in her existence. In addition to the resources which
were common to Denver and are now to Salt Lake, the latter city
has, as a very potent factor to her future growth and development, the wonderful Salt Lake and her other splendid summer
attractions and health resorts, which will make this city
second to no other in the country, as a place to which the
wealthy and the intelligent people of our country will make
their regular pilgrimages. Salt Lake City is beginning to rival
some of the better known summer resorts in the extreme
Northern states and on the Atlantic Coast, for the reason that
all of the attractions to be found separately at these various
summer resorts can be found in close proximity and of
superior character within an hour's ride of Salt Lake City.
Even now, wealthy people from different parts of the country
are erecting summer cottages on the Lake, or in the mountains
close by Salt Lake, and in a few years, without any question,
the Great Salt Lake of Utah, with its unrivalled attractions of
beautiful mountain scenery, delightful and invigorating bathing, splendid boating and sailing, will rival, in the number of
its resorts, extent of its hotels and beauty of its cottages, lakes
Minnetonka and Oconomowoc.

Salt Lake City with its remarkable medicinal and thermal
springs will be the Saratoga of the West, and for its mountain
trout fishing, delightful camping and hunting, will have no
superior anywhere in the country.

There is no place to which the tourist or pleasure or health
seeker can turn with greater assurance of finding all of the
attractions for which he could wish, and will be afforded him,
than are to be found here.

Salt Lake City's municipal affairs are conducted upon a
broad gauge but an entirely economical basis. Her total
assessed valuation of $16,611,752 is only about one-fifth of the
actual value of the property it represents. Her rate of
valuation for city purposes is no greater than for territorial

purposes.   Her total rate for general taxation is only one cent and seven mills on each dollar of assessed valuation.

With a total of sixteen banks and a capital of over $4,000,000 —on May 1st, 1890, Salt Lake is the strongest financial city of her size in this country.

· With two well conducted morning and two well conducted evening papers, and some twenty other papers, the press of Salt Lake City is well represented, and does the city much effective work.

ECHO ROCK.

CHAPTER IV

THE FUTURE OF SALT LAKE CITY.

TO the seeker after investments, profits, or a business location, no city presents more variety or greater assurance of success than does Salt Lake City. At no time in the history of this country has there been an instance of any city which possessed greater certainty of a grand future than does Salt Lake City to-day. Her location is most fortunate, but her immediate possibilities and prospects, to be fully appreciated, must be investigated. Situated as she is, in the very heart of this great Inter Mountain country, with railroad communications to all portions that have been in any way developed, and with other lines to undeveloped parts of the same in contemplation and construction, Salt Lake City occupies a position which has given her absolute control of this great Inter Mountain country, as its metropolis.

Taking Utah as a basis, with her 250,000 people, and her wealth of 127,000,000 of dollars, Salt Lake also has naturally tributary to her all the vast resources of northern Arizona, Nevada, southeastern Oregon, Idaho, western Wyoming and western Colorado, a country in extent unequalled by that which is tributary to any other one city in the United States. That this vast and wonderful country needs a metropolis, and that Salt Lake City is destined to be that metropolis, are settled and established facts. The hidden wealth with which these mountains teem, will be a constant source of revenue to Salt Lake—constant because these precious metals are to be found and to be developed at any time of any year, day or night, simply by the application of the rapidly improving methods for developing the same. This wealth is not susceptible of eradication by such fickle elements as lack of rain, hot winds, or destructive pests. The development of these

GUNNISON'S BUTTE.

resources will create and sustain a most desirable market for a large and highly prosperous agricultural and industrial community, and by reason of the great cost of importing across the mountains surrounding this Inter Mountain country, agricultural productions and manufactured goods, there are afforded in this section unexcelled advantages for agriculture, for manufacturing, and for industrial enterprises. These various elements in the makeup of this Inter Mountain country blend harmoniously, and provide mutually beneficial trade relations.

The mineral resources of Utah in particular, and of this Inter Mountain country in general, cannot be appreciated, much less estimated, as their development is yet only in its infancy, as are also the agricultural resources of the section named. All are mutually beneficial to each other. That Salt Lake City will develop as rapidly and as greatly as has Denver, is readily apparent to any one who will investigate the relative resources of the two cities. When Denver was the present size of Salt Lake City, about 50,000, she had, as her own territory, a country comprising Wyoming, Colorado and New Mexico, with mineral wealth only upon one side of her territory, and with a much more limited agricultural and grazing country than that which surrounds Salt Lake in all directions, as do also her wonderful mineral resources. By the time Salt Lake's tributary territory has been developed to the degree that Denver's tributary territory is at the present time, the resources and the products of the former will, by careful estimation of practical men, be fully twice as great as are those of the latter city's territory. As a consequence there is every certainty of the constant and rapid development of Salt Lake City into a metropolis equaling, if not excelling, the proud record made by the wonderful city on the eastern slope of the Rocky Mountains.

Almost every known mineral or mineral product which can be utilized in the arts and sciences is to be found in Utah, and

TROUT POOL OGDEN CANON.

in the adjacent states and territories; and in such quantities and so located as to be susceptible of development and practical application. For the utilization of these products used in the lines of manufacturing, Salt Lake City presents the greatest possible advantages. She has in easy reach, great bodies of iron ore of a high grade and veins of coal, which for coking and general manufacturing purposes are not excelled by even the famous Connellsville coal and coke. For manufacturing purposes of a lighter nature than those which require such large quantities of fuel for smelting and refining purposes, there has been organized in this city a company which will furnish to consumers, at purely nominal cost, fuel gas for lighting, heating and for manufacturing purposes.

Another source of developing power for industrial purposes and generating light for domestic and public uses, is found in the great amount of water power in the several creeks which empty out of the mountain cañons into the valley of the Great Salt Lake at and near Salt Lake City. This power is practically inexhaustible, and can be easily utilized and turned to great profit, not only to the city, but to the promoters of such an enterprise as would develop the same. This matter has been given a thorough investigation by experts, and pronounced entirely feasible. A company is now forming in this city for the purpose of utilizing this power.

The sources of small and diversified industries already in operation here, the electric street railways, and electric light companies, etc., etc., already provide ample opportunity for disposing of such power at profitable figures, which is not the case in any other city in this great Inter Mountain country.

Already there are daily accessions to the industrial and commercial institutions of Salt Lake City, each one of which aids in strengthening Salt Lake's position as the metropolis of the territory indicated.

CHAPTER V.

GREAT SALT LAKE.

TO persons in search of pleasure no more delightful place can be found than Salt Lake City, which without **exaggeration** excels all **other places** in point of variety, diversity and excellent character of its various kinds of recreation and summer resorts, to be found anywhere. There is no other city in this country which has such a variety of summer attractions so ready of access. At the Great Salt Lake which is only thirty minutes ride from the city, is to be found salt water bathing excelling that at the Atlantic or Pacific seaside resorts. There are two beautiful and thoroughly equipped bathing resorts, of which Lake Park on the Rio Grande Western Railroad is the one most easy of access and which possesses unexcelled attractions. By the beginning of the season there will be opened two more first class resorts for the accommodation of the rapidly increasing crowds, who daily throng the beautiful white-sanded beaches of this inland sea. The Great Salt Lake is 120 miles in length by 60 miles at its greatest width. It is surrounded by beautiful mountains and dotted with picturesque islands of various sizes, the largest containing about thirty thousand acres. Pleasure boats of all sorts and descriptions ply upon the lake and afford diversion for the numerous visitors to this great summer resort. The popularity of these resorts is evidenced by the fact, that more than a quarter of a million of people avail themselves of the pleasures of a bath in Salt Lake during the season, between the middle of May and the middle of September. The specific gravity of these waters is about seventeen per cent. greater than that of the Atlantic Ocean's waters, and they carry in solution, according to the season of the year, from eighteen to twenty-two per cent. of salt. During the mid-summer afternoons and evenings these waters are almost lukewarm, and a bath after

CASTLE GATE.

business hours is not only restful and invigorating but has also the effect of a tonic. The popularity of this great resort has only begun, but without doubt, as its superior attractions become more generally known it will secure deserved recognition as one of the leading summer resorts of the United States and must become a strong rival to the more expensive places of a similar character upon our seaboards.

The mysterious characteristics of this great inland sea appeal strongly to the imagination. In this connection the following verses by W. E. Pabor may be very appropriately quoted·

> Over the Oquirrh ranges
>   Pearly clouds of softness rest,
> Blending with the rippling changes
>   On great Salt Lake's wave swept breast.
> In the sunset I am roaming,
>   Looking out across the deep
> Tideless waves that in the gloaming
>   Moan as if in dreamy sleep.
>
> Locked in the embrace of mountains,
>   Whose green frontlets watch the isles,
> Guarding the enchanted fountains
>   Where a siren sits and smiles.
> Lake of mystery and wonder,
>   Lake of silence so sublime,
> In thy depths we look and ponder
>   On the strangest gift of time.
>
> Lower down the crimson chamber
>   Of the west the sunset falls ;
> Creamy cumuli of amber
>   Fenciled on its crystal walls;
> Now the tints change into umber,
>   Twilight shadows creep along
> Slowly, like the sense of slumber,
>   Through the solace of a song.

GREAT SALT LAKE.

As the sunset's charm thrills through me,
  Musing on the sand-swept marge,
Fancy brings a boatman to me
  With his pearl-enameled barge;
And he bids me leave the highlands,
  With their shadow and their stain,
And sail with him to the islands
  Lying in the azure main.

Farewell now to all things human
  In the boatman's barge I stand,
Trust of man or love of woman
  I leave on the shore of sand.
Through empurpled mists that hover
  Round the islands of the blest,
In the sunset I go over
  To the lotus land of rest.

The lake has an area of 2,500 square miles and its surface is higher than the Alleghany Mountains. Its mean depth is about 60 feet and numerous small islands ornament its bosom, the principal of which are the Antelope and the Stanbury. At different periods the level of the lake has changed and re-changed most perceptibly, which has led scientists to conjecture that the shore land was by no means stable. It compares with other bodies of saline water analytically as follows:

	WATER.	SOLIDS
Atlantic Ocean	96 5	3.5
Mediterranean	96.2	3.8
Dead Sea	76.0	24.0
Great Salt Lake	86.0	14.0

In specific gravity, distilled waterybeing unity, the followin comparison exists:

Ocean Water	10.27
Dead Sea	11.16
Great Salt Lake	11.07

LAKE PARK.

This feature of a summer resort, together with the splendid fresh water boating and bathing which are afforded at Utah Lake, (a splendid body of fresh water containing 125 square miles, and only an hour's ride south of the city by rail,) and the delightful hunting, fishing and camping in the mountains immediately surrounding Salt Lake City, make her the most desirable summer resort to be found anywhere. There is no other city to be named which possesses in so great a degree the diversity of resorts and recreations that are to be found immediately accessible to Salt Lake City. And this fact alone is the source of great profit to Salt Lake City, which can grow and develop as a summer resort in the same degree that St. Paul and Minneapolis grew upon the strength of the summer attractions of which they were the commercial centers.

After a day spent so pleasantly at the beach, the pleasure seeker can return to the city and enjoy the cool, bracing atmosphere of the Salt Lake summer night. Should he desire to wile away a few pleasant hours by a drive about the city, or into the beautiful cañons close by, or to attend the theatre or the opera, and witness the presentation of the standard stage attractions by the first class companies of the country, he will have that privilege, as this city with its Grand Opera house and the Salt Lake theatre is recognized as the greatest amusement place of its size in the country.

CHAPTER VI.

THE CITY OF OGDEN.

THE City of Ogden is one of the most beautiful towns in America. It is one of the oldest settlements in Utah, and has now attained the dignity of quite a metropolitan city with 20,000 inhabitants. It is the key to the railroad situation in the Inter Mountain region, and has the trackage and terminals of the seven railroads at present in the Territory. As a place of residence Ogden has few peers. It nestles at the base of the Wasatch Mountains, several of whose peaks reach an altitude of nearly two miles above sea level and tower one mile above the city. From Salt Lake City to Ogden there is a regular procession of villages with Great Salt Lake plainly in sight on the west and the glorious Wasatch range rising in majestic grandeur on the east. One is given an entrancing view of the city and its environs immediately upon arriving at the handsome new Union depot. The picture is one that never tires the eye or ceases to appeal to the sense of beauty. The mountains rise abruptly from the eastern and northern limits of the city like guardian sentinels shielding the people from the cold blasts of the north and the rasping, bone searching currents from the east. The city gently slopes from the foot of the mountains west towards the great lake, its western lines reaching within a short distance of those briny waters that are so near the point of saturation that nothing that has life can exist in them. Two rivers flow through the city. The Ogden and the Weber. These generous streams pour from two cañons with similar names. They are celebrated trout streams, attracting hundreds of visitors every year who "whip" them for miles, and are rewarded by generous "catches" of speckled beauties that gamely rise to the fly.

Ogden Cañon is directly east of the city. The water in

GATE OF LODORE.

this cañon is as pure and sparkling as any water ever
quaffed by man. From this store of living waters drained from
the heart of the mountains the city gets its supply of water for
all purposes. It is in abundance throughout the year, irrigating countless acres of the most fertile land in the world, after
supplying the city with liquid comfort. Standing on the elevated
plateau east of the city one has a splendid view of a most
delightful panorama, composed of mountain, lake, valley, city
and sky, that has to be seen to be fully enjoyed. There is
probably no spot on earth where all the elements of a most
lovely picture are more markedly present. It seems that in
this beautiful city, that was only a raw village a few years ago,
is combined the essentials for the prosperity and happiness of
men. It is in the midst of a most lovely and fertile region
watered by several of the most romantic and bounteous rivers
in the Rockies. It has an atmosphere that is almost incom-
parable, a wealth of mineral beyond computation and a
population filled with energy, business pluck and broad gauge
effort. The varied beauty of the Salt Lake Valley is almost
magical. The great American Dead Sea is the central piece
of the picture as viewed from the heights about Ogden. It is
so near the city that one feels he can walk to it in a few
minutes. Its bold islands and fringes of noble mountains stand
out in blue-toned beauty, capped with eternal snow. In the
north and south are stretches of lovely valley and glimpses of
lofty mountains, whose snow-wrapped peaks loom softly against
the blue background of rare and bracing air. On specially
clear days one can see dimly outlined in the far, far west the
hazy forms of the Sierra Nevada Mountains. The valley is
equal in beauty to the famous vale of Cashmere, and is as fertile
as the wildest imagination can conceive. It is one vast stretch
of farm, garden and orchard, watered by musical streams and
dotted with pretty villages and farm houses. The city is about
four miles square. It is laid off at right angles. The streets are

broad and well shaded by umbrageous trees, kept in splendid condition by the sparkling mountain water that is in abundance in every part of the town. The dwellings of the people are pretty and many of them large and stylish. It does the eye of the traveler good to ride through the city and look at the lovely lawns and beautiful flowers. In the spring the air of the residence part of the town is permeated with the odor of violets and new mown grass. In the summer the abundance of roses and other flowers perfume the atmosphere, while all around are trees and shrubbery rejoicing in a wealth of tender foliage. The city has several parks well set in trees and beautiful grasses, whose smooth lawns invite to repose and refreshment during the warm months. The drives in and about Ogden are very fine. But the people are engaged in building a boulevard this summer that will scarcely find an equal in the world. It will reach from the lake east to Ogden Cañon and up that grand gorge for eight or nine miles. The length of this superb drive will be about twenty miles. For the most part of its length the boulevard will command the view of valley, lake and mountain above mentioned. The business part of the city is well built and fully equipped to supply the needs of the vast stretch of agricultural and mineral country tributary to it. There is a large retail and wholesale trade centered here, which is increasing at a rate that indicates a great future for this beautiful mountain city.

Nature has done a great deal for Ogden and its immediate neighborhood. Within a few miles of the city, easy of access, are beautiful and shady parks where a whole day or afternoon can be passed enjoyably. North of the city are the Wasatch Mountains whose snow-capped peaks are glorious to gaze upon, radiant in the interchangeable garb of green and purple. These mountains loom skyward thousands of feet, and intermingle with the clouds, presenting a sight that is indeed enchanting. From the top of Ogden Mountain, the highest

COLD WATER CANON.

of the range, the country for hundreds of miles around is
pictured to the observer with a clearness and distinctness that
when objects a hundred miles away are pointed out and the
distance stated, words of surprise and astonishment escape
from the lips of the entranced beholder. These mountains
besides furnishing such excellent views and means of observa-
tion supply many attractions for the geologist and seeker after
curiosities. They are prolific of minerals of every variety,
and with little difficulty beyond the tax of stooping over, the

explorer can become supplied with an abundance of handsome specimens of minerals designed to beautify the parlor or ornament the sitting and dining room.

In the very heart of the Wasatch range of mountains is Ogden Cañon, nine miles in length, which is an entrancing spot and adapted by nature to cause the visitor to gaze in perfect astonishment. A beautiful driveway and footpath traverses the entire distance through the cañon, which has few superiors, if it has any at all, for the stateliness of the mountains, its rush of waters and its manifold attractions. The magnificent mountains towering thousands of feet high are beautiful to behold. In many places the formations are chiseled and carved out through exposure to the elements in manners to instill one with the belief that it had been done by human hands. The cañon is a favorite resort for the people of Ogden and tourists, and all hours throughout the day the road through it is lined with people on foot and in vehicles admiring and enjoying the greatest of giants of Nature's own gift. The roar of the restless waters of the great falls as they empty into the Ogden River strikes the visitor with awe, and their turbulency and swiftness are equal to the rapids of the famous St. Lawrence River. This vast fall of water is soon to be utilized. The Ogden Power Company, recently organized through the efforts of one of the leading business men and capitalists of Ogden, is now building great works in the cañon for the purpose of storing the water to be utilized for driving the machinery in all parts of the city by electricity. The stock is owned by Ogden and San Francisco capitalists to the amount of $250,000. It is a great work and one that future generations will thank its originator for having handed down to them. The water is also intended to furnish power for manufacturers, and electric street railways which are projected and will soon be in operation.

Among the innumerable attractions of the cañon is the hot springs, which are located near its mouth. The water is suffi-

FALLS IN WHEELER'S CANON.

ciently temperate to make bathing agreeable and pleasant.
The baths are free to everyone and are liberally patronized and
beneficial results are invariably the case.   At times the wind
blows down the cañon at the rate of sixty miles an hour, and
one caught in one of these gales enjoys an experience that is
exhilarating and wildly exciting.   It is a pleasant excitement
though and in the exuberance that immediately takes posses-
sion of the sightseer induces him or her, to greatly enjoy the
flurry.   The great rapids lash and splash, and their roar can
be heard high above the murmurings of the wind.   They
appear to laugh with merriment as they dash their cool and
invigorating spray into the faces of those perambulating the
banks of the stream.   No pen can describe the grandeur and
weirdness of Ogden Cañon.   It must be seen in a leisurely
way to be thoroughly appreciated.

The winters in the valley are not long and the cold is pleasantly tempered by the air from the lake. Although Ogden is
4,300 feet above sea level it rarely experiences very low temperature. In the hot months the heat is tempered by mountain
breezes and the salt air from the lake. The nights are uniformly
cool and pleasant. These facts, with its perfect drainage, broad
and splendidly shaded streets, pure and delicious water, render
it the delight of the tourist and the happy residence of a busy
and prosperous people.

The valley is wonderfully productive from a point ten miles
north of Ogden away south of Salt Lake City. The farms in
this tract of country are among the most valuable acre property
in the world. But the extreme northern end of the valley has
heretofore been scantily tilled, owing to the difficulty of get-
ting water on the lands. This blot on an otherwise magnificent
region is now in a fair way to be wiped out. About one year
ago some capitalists conceived the design of a great canal to
irrigate this country, something like 500,000 acres. They
organized and stocked an enterprise called the Bear River
Canal Company, bonded it for $2,000,000, surveyed the route
and through contractors started the work last summer. Bear
Lake is a beautiful sheet of water in the Wasatch Mountains
forty-five miles north of Ogden. The water in this lake,
which is six by thirty miles in extent, is of great depth and
pureness. It is supplied by mountain streams and springs and
pours its surplus water into Bear River. This river winds its tor-
tuous course through the cañon to and across Salt Lake Valley,
and finally pours its waters into the great Dead Sea of America.
The waters of the river are of great volume and inexhaustible.
The plan contemplates two canals, one on each side of the
river. The west branch debouches from the Bear River Cañon
and is to irrigate the lands lying at the northern end of the
valley and about the northern arms of the Great Salt Lake.
The east branch winds along the high bench at the western

BUTTES OF THE CROSS.

base of the Wasatch range, and is to supply the land as far south as Ogden, where, if there be no use for the surplus water brought to this point, it will be suffered to run into the Ogden River. The work is well under way with a fine prospect of being finished before next winter. It is probable that no similar work of its magnitude and physical difficulty has ever been undertaken in the United States. In order to shorten distance it has been necessary to tunnel hills, blast down solid rocks and excavate millions of tons of earth on mountain sides.

This stupendous enterprise has challenged attention all over the country. Its successful completion will be a triumph for American brain and financial pluck. It will reclaim land that now produces only sage brush and scant wild grasses, and which will be worth from $2,000,000 to $25,000,000. It is estimated that the reclaimed land will support a farming population of more than 100,000 souls and will soon be thrown open to settlement. As a sort of supplement to the irrigation scheme the company has contracted with the city of Ogden to

supply the city with a new and extensive water system capable
of furnishing water for a city of nearly 200,000 people. The
work of laying the mains will be completed at an early date
this summer.

In close proximity to Ogden, and easy of access, are many
attractions and pleasant resorts for excursion parties, and in
the proper season they are extensively patronized. An enjoy-
able spot, where one can find quick and permanent relief and
cure for the many maladies the human form is heir to, is the
Utah Hot Springs nine miles distant from Ogden. The waters
are thoroughly impregnated with iron and other health
restoring minerals, and pour forth in great volumes from the
earth at a temperature of 125 degrees. They are quite salt,
but not unpleasant to the taste, and but few people are able to
undergo the first bath owing to the intense warmth of the
waters. However, the bather quickly becomes accustomed to
the waters, and the place is furnished with every convenience
to assure the comfort and enjoyment of the patron. The
waters contain such ingredients as chloride of sodium, iron,
magnesia and nitre, in strong solution, and for rheumatic
troubles and blood diseases cannot be surpassed. Additional
improvements are contemplated, and men will be put at work
shortly improving the already handsome hotel. Near by the
springs is a mile track, which is the finest and speediest in the
country, and a summer meeting for large purses will be held.

The country around Ogden is wonderfully productive. The
lands yield in wheat from 40 to 80 bushels to the acre and
other cereal crops in proportion. The hay crop is immense
and pays handsomely. Farmers manage to cut three crops of
alfalfa each season. The country in this part of the valley is
also a great fruit growing region. Peaches, pears, apples,
grapes, apricots, etc., do exceedingly well, and the fruit is of a
delicious flavor. The yield in potatoes is almost beyond belief.
It is a common thing for the best lands to produce from 600
to 800 bushels to the acre, while the most indifferent soil easily

EARLY MORNING ON OGDEN RIVER.

produces 400 bushels per acre.   The market for all the products of the valley is found in the numerous cities and
mining camps of Utah and neighboring states and territories.
The prices realized are always good, which insures the farmer
good returns for his labor.   All crops are raised by irrigation.
Such a thing as crop failure has never been known in the
valley.

CHAPTER VII.

SCENERY OF UTAH.

T HE scenery of Utah is grand and picturesque, abound-
ing in strong contrasts and startling changes. Mountain and valley, lake and forest, alternate in bewildering
beauty. As one approaches from the East via the Denver &
Rio Grande Railroad the scenery is wonderfully varied and
attractive. In a book devoted to Utah it would hardly be ap-
propriate to describe at length the scenery on the Rio Grande
Railroad in Colorado, but those who approach Salt Lake City
or Ogden from the east will have the pleasure of passing
through this scenery, including the Royal Gorge, Grand Cañon
of the Arkansas, Marshall Pass and Black Cañon, and will
have the privilege of beholding Pike's Peak, the Collegiate
Range, the Sangre de Cristo and Mounts Ouray and Shaveno
—therefore, this brief mention may not be considered out of
place.

At Grand Junction the Gunnison River joins the Grand,
which flows through a fertile valley where numerous farms have
been located and a considerable city has grown up. A few
miles beyond Grand Junction the Colorado line is passed and
the traveler is in Utah, and the railroad is under the manage-
ment of the Rio Grande Western Company. The scenery for
the next hundred miles has grandeur enough in variety to make
it interesting. The Book Cliffs, which are a richly colored and
peculiar formation, are followed for some distance, while to the
southward rise the snowy groups of the Sierra la Sal and San
Rafael Mountains. Green River, which goes to form the Rio
Colorado, is soon passed with its swift flowing current which
comes from far up in the Yellowstone Park and finally mingles,
after wandering 2,000 miles, with the waters of the Pacific.

OGDEN CANON LOOKING WEST.   GREAT SALT LAKE IN THE DISTANCE.

From where the road crosses Green River, may be seen in the distance the summits of the broken walls that form the grand cañon of the Colorado fifty miles away. Soon the peaks of the Wasatch rise beyond Castle Valley. The scenery becomes more picturesque and the beautiful in nature again appears as we approach Castle gate at the entrance of Price river cañon. This bold and striking rock formation is similar in many respects to the gateway of the Garden of the Gods. The two huge pillars or ledges of rock composing it are offshoots of the cliffs behind. They are of different heights, one measuring five hundred and the other four hundred and fifty feet from top to base. They are richly dyed with red and the firs and pines growing about them, but reaching only to their lower strata, render this coloring more noticeable and beautiful. Between the two sharp promontories, which are separated only by a narrow space, the river and the railroad both run, one pressing closely against the other. The stream leaps over a rocky bed and its banks are lined with tangled brush. The turreted rocks, the rushing stream and the darkling cañon bring forcibly to mind that wonderful dream of Coleridge:

> "In Xanadu did Kubla Khan
> A stately pleasure-dome decree;
> Where Alph, the sacred river, ran
> Through caverns measureless to man.
> Down to a sunless sea.
> So twice five miles of fertile ground
> With walls and towers were girdled round;
> And here were gardens bright with sinuous rills,
> Where blossom'd many an incense-bearing tree;
> And here were forests ancient as the hills,
> Infolding sunny spots of greenery."

Once past the gate, and looking back, the bold headlands forming it have a new and more attractive beauty. They are higher and more massive, it seems, than when we were in their shadow. Huge rocks project far out from their perpendicular

WINNIE'S GROTTO.

faces.   No other isolated pinnacles in this region approach them in size or majesty.   They are landmarks up and **down the** cañon, their lofty tops catching the eye before their **bases are** discovered

The impression made by these remarkable monoliths **is best** conveyed by the following poem:

" Stand, stranger, stand.   The castle gate
Through which you pass to fairy land
Is mine to guard.   What happy fate
Bids you within its border ?   Stand!"

Warder of this stately castle,
Stay the menace of your hand,
I am but a simple singer
Singing songs throughout the land.
Through the time-stained rugged portals
I can catch a glimpse afar,
Where the light shines on the woodland
Like the light of the morning star.

Let me pass, O, stern-faced warder,
Through the wondrous castle gate;
Let me walk within the garden
Led by fancy and by fate.
For the sunlight and the moonlight
And the starlight, as they fall,
Seem replete with happy fancies
Making pictures on the wall.

Gateway to a happy valley,
Open wide and let my feet
Wander in the flowery meadows
Where the shining waters meet.
Frowning cliffs lift up to front me,
Sunset hues the rocks that rise,
But my eyes have caught a vision
Of green fields and violet skies.

Lying over Soldier Summit
  In the valley of the West,
With the bloom and blush of **Eden**
  Lying softly on their breast,
Vales of splendor, vales of beauty,
  Meet to melt a heart of stone;
Vale of Tempe pales in glory
  When beside thy brightness shown.

Other lips have uttered fancies,
  Other eyes on thee have shone,
Other feet have walked these meadows,
  Passing through the gate of **stone.**
But my lips can not keep silence,
  Or my eyes their rapture bate,
As they catch a glimpse of Eden
Through the cliff crowned Castle Gate.

" Pass, stranger, **pass,** the olden **time**
  Was full of song **of** mirth **and cheer;**
Sing any song that suits your rhyme,
  And let it echo round the year."

Beyond the gateway weird and fantastic ,rock formations
abound like bastions, battlements and castles. Rock pinnacles
rise on every hand in massive majesty. The road runs along
the banks of the river which is never lost sight of. A well-
worn wagon road follows the cañon, and it was through this
pass that Albert Sydney Johnston led his army on his return
from Utah. The scene is one to delight the eye of the artist
as the shadows gather in the depths of the cañon and the sun
gilds the towering heights. Through Spanish Peak, a depres-
sion in the range, one can see the heights of Mount Nebo over-
looking the " Promised Land," and suddenly, the train darting
out into the Utah valley, there lies spread out before the traveler the land which the Mormons have made to blossom as the
rose. It is a scene of Arcadian beauty, as the setting sun
rests upon the meadow lands the tinkle of the cowbells is
heard. The train rolls rapidly by thrifty farm houses, fields

WATERFALL CANON.

green with alfalfa, across irrigating ditches that make peren-
nial spring time.

Utah Lake lies in the center of the valley of the same name.
It is a picturesque sheet of clear, fresh water, to the north of
which lie the Mormon towns of Provo and Springville. The
scene is an entrancing one. Eastward the oblong basin is
shut in by the Wasatch mountains, and on the West is the

Oquirrh Range.   Northward are low hills, or mesas, crossing the valley and separating it from that of the Great Salt Lake, while in the south, the east and west ranges approach each other and form blue-tinted walls of uneven shape.   To the left of this barrier, Mount Nebo, highest and grandest of the Utah peaks, rises majestically above all surroundings.   Its summit sparkles with snow, and its lower slopes are wooded and soft, while from it and extending north and south run vast, broken vari-colored confreres.   The valley is like a well-kept garden; farm joins farm; crystal streams water it, and scattered about in rich profusion are long lines of fruit trees, amid which are trim white houses.   Salt Lake City is visible and beyond slumber the waters of the Great Salt Lake.

The scenery of the Great Salt Lake and that between Salt Lake City and Ogden, including the cañons and mountains in that vicinity, have been described in another place, therefore, suffice it to say that for variety, beauty and grandeur the scenery of Utah is unrivalled.

www.ingramcontent.com/pod-product-compliance
Lightning Source LLC
Chambersburg PA
CBHW031759090426
42739CB00008B/1078